Winterberries and Apple Blossoms

REFLECTIONS AND FLAVORS OF A MENNONITE YEAR

Winterberries & Apple Blossoms

REFLECTIONS AND FLAVORS OF A MENNONITE YEAR

By NAN FORLER   *Paintings by* PETER ETRIL SNYDER

TUNDRA BOOKS

Published in Canada by Tundra Books,
75 Sherbourne Street, Toronto, Ontario M5A 2P9

Published in the United States by Tundra Books of Northern New York,
P.O. Box 1030, Plattsburgh, New York 12901

Library of Congress Control Number: 2011922762

LIBRARY AND ARCHIVES CANADA CATALOGUING IN PUBLICATION

Forler, Nan
        Winterberries and apple blossoms : reflections and flavors of a Mennonite year / by Nan Forler ; paintings by Peter Etril Snyder.

Poems.
ISBN 978-1-77049-254-7

        1. Mennonites--Juvenile poetry. 2. Mennonite cooking--Juvenile literature.
I. Snyder, Peter Etril, 1944- II. Title.

PS8611.O76W56 2011   jC811'.6   C2011-901224-3

We acknowledge the financial support of the Government of Canada through the Book Publishing Industry Development Program (BPIDP) and that of the Government of Ontario through the Ontario Media Development Corporation's Ontario Book Initiative. We further acknowledge the support of the Canada Council for the Arts and the Ontario Arts Council for our publishing program.

ONTARIO ARTS COUNCIL
CONSEIL DES ARTS DE L'ONTARIO

The paintings for this book were rendered in acrylics on masonite
Design: Andrew Roberts / Jennifer Lum
Printed and bound in Singapore

1 2 3 4 5 6   16 15 14 13 12 11

The child-friendly recipes in this book have been coded for their degree of difficulty. All children should have adult supervision when the use of sharp implements, the oven, or stove-top is required.

For my mother, Elaine Forler, and my grandmother, Alma Dillon,
in whose kitchens I learned about baking and life,
and for Kevin, Dillon, and Maia, always.
– N.F.

To my bride, Marilyn.
– P.E.S.

Reflections

Naomi is a young girl who has been raised in the Old Order Mennonite Community. Faithfully abiding by the rules of her church, she lives a simple life with very few modern conveniences and worldly possessions.

There are no computers, no cars, no televisions, no fancy clothes. Naomi spends her time helping her mother in the house, doing chores on the farm, and playing outside with her brothers and sisters.

Naomi's first language is an unwritten German dialect called Pennsylvania Dutch. She attends school in a one-room, country schoolhouse with other children who share her beliefs and customs. Naomi and her family strive to live modestly and in keeping with the teachings of the Bible.

Winterberries and Apple Blossoms is a glimpse into one year of Naomi's plain and peaceful life.

THE QUILTING BEE

Matilda Martin and Edna Bauman,
Mam and Lucinda and me –
my first time quilting with the women.
Noisy greetings as we settle in around the quilt frame,
then silence as each begins.

Only the pop of needles through sky-blue cotton,
the creak of the wooden frame,
horses clopping snow from their hooves
against the icy laneway outside.

And then it starts again,
the clatter and chatter of women, the laughter, the talk –
Lucinda scolding me to keep my stitches even,
while hungry needles scoop up fabric
in tiny, equal bites.

That night, I crawl into bed beneath another quilt –
from another winter, other chatter –
wondering what stories this quilt has heard,
and who will be warmed by the one we're making.

I press my cold feet against my sister's legs;
she grumbles and rolls away.
Back to back, heavy with dreaming,
I tuck my toes beneath her legs,
and run my fingers over rows of stitches,
counting them to sleep.

THE GENERAL STORE

We follow close behind Mam,
Esther tugging on the edges of her long black shawl,
running to keep up,
past a freezer lined with hard snow
and filled with frosty meat and ice-cream cartons,
past boxes of dark shirts and bonnets,
bags of broken maple leaf cookies and orange drink powder,
cake mix, straw hats, moth balls and bobby pins,
homemade soap and sponge toffee,
stacked to the ceiling.
Reaching for a can of peas
might make the whole shelf tumble.

I pause at the rack of toys
and peer up
at the same yellow-haired doll
that's been hanging there forever,
dusty and alone.
"Now then, Naomi, you're too old.
You don't need it no more. Come now!"

Creaky stairs lead to the fabric room and a section
of blue:
blue gingham, blue flowers, sky blue, the blue of a robin's egg.
I pull out a bolt of blue lilacs, plump flowers
with delicately painted petals,

and imagine a dress.

My mother reaches across
to a bolt of plain navy blue.
"This should do for you now, Naomi,
for church-going,"
and asks for three yards.

By the cash register,
I peer at the View-Master cards with one eye open,
white cardboard circles with miniature pictures
of places far away:
the Grand Canyon, Niagara Falls, China.
I hold the package close,
trying to see the world
in the tiny, dark squares.

Picking up the bag of navy cloth,
I follow my mother.

March

THE SUGAR BUSH

Sploosh, sploosh.
The brown-sugar slush collapses
into pale water beneath my boots.
Swinging my lunch pail,
I make my way along the path to the sugar bush.

My feet sink into wet holes as I run
to the first tree I see tapped.
I press my tongue against the cold spile,
to catch the dangling sweet sap
before it plinks into the silver metal bucket.
"Naom!" Dat calls harshly.
"You should be going home, not?"

I hide behind the woodpile.
Listening to the fire crack and crackle,
I peer over the graying wood
to see my father, Manassah, and David
dumping buckets of sap into a huge black pot.
The air above is wavy,
as if I'm looking at them
through a bottle of oil.

David, the hired boy, sees me.
I duck down
then
slowly
raise
my head
above the woodpile again.
He is still looking my way.
He smiles.
I drop to the ground.

Crouched in the wet snow,
I close my eyes
and breathe in
the woodburning-mapley-sweet air,
tasting spring through my nose.

PICKING STONES

If we do not praise Him, the rocks will cry out.
I draw an outline around the base of the stone
and pluck it from the ground,
leaving behind a perfect print.
The stone clunks into the skirt of my apron.
I lug my pile to the cart.
"Six more," I sigh, my back hunched
and aching,
but no one else is counting.
Across the field, Jonah hollers. "Big one!"
Manassah brings a board.
We all help to pry the boulder from its bed
   Not a stone shall be left unturned.
and carry it to the cart.

Stones missed will choke the crops
   Some seeds fell on rocky soil…
Manassah points and pulls up close.
Hop off the moving wagon,
claw for stones,
run to catch up.

An endless day.
I stare up at the sky, wiped gray
with dirty clouds.
Manassah announces we'll head for the bush.
The best part.

Standing on the cart,
we throw
the stones into the trees.
   Let the one without sin cast the first stone.
Yellow dog-toothed violets hang their heads.

A raindrop splats on my arm.
Manassah dumps the remaining stones
as we hurry for home,
our dusty dresses now soaked in mud.

The house is warm
with brown sugar and molasses —
shoo-fly pies in the oven.
We pull chairs up to the table
for hot cider and board games.
I flick the crokinole button,
my fingers black with earth,
my hands scratched and raw.
   The Lord is my rock, my fortress.

THE BICYCLE

The boys glide past on their bicycles,
looking back, teasing.
Boys on bikes, girls on foot.
Esther swings her lunchbox,
not bothered by their *schputting*
and their shiny wheels.

Ahead of us, they stop
and rest their bikes on the road,
tearing off toward the rhubarb patch
for a sour snack before school.

I reach down, prop up Jonah's bike
and motion for Esther to keep walking.
How Mam would scold:
"Imagine, one of my daughters …"
And yet…
hiking up my dress,
I swing my leg over the seat,
push down on the pedal.
A soft thud beneath my foot,
and the wheels begin to turn.
At first, a wobbly struggle.

And then,
the bike and me,
the sun, the breeze on my face,
my braids whipping my back,
my skirt flapping – caught
in the chain.

The bike and me
crash to the gravel.

I look back to the rhubarb patch
(no one has seen),
and rip my skirt out of the greasy chain,
picking out the extra bits of navy fabric
left behind
and stuffing them in my shoe.
I wipe my eyes on my sleeve,
brush the gravel from my legs,
and hurry to catch up with Esther.

She holds my hand.
Blood seeps through my stockings,
coloring the knees purply black,
as we carry on to school,
our heads held high.

ICE CREAM

The sun is hot,
the morning – long.
Manassah, Lucinda, Jonah, and Esther,
the hired boy David, and me.
With red-stained hands, we pluck
the nodding berries, juicy and plump,
from their shaded beds.
Esther's pail is almost empty,
her chin dripping with juice.

"Ice cream!" someone shouts.
We drop our berry baskets and run.
Salty ice shushes and tumbles
against the wooden ice-cream pail.
Dat pours leftover sugar and cream into a coffee tin,
sets it in a can of ice, seals the lid, and hands it to me.
I hug the can, feeling the cool metal
through my dress.

"Get her!" Manassah shouts.
David chases after me,
trying to snatch the can,
teasing.
I laugh and grab his arm,
pretending to hand it over,
then push him away.

We take turns
kicking the can over the grass.
I jump and skip, whirling
like the cream in the can,
filled with the thrill of it.

Flushed and out of breath,
I hurry away from the boys
back to Dat.

The ice-cream crank stiffens and stops.
The silver metal canister,
sweaty with cold,
emptied into bowls.
Icy, white, creamy, vanilla
ice cream.

Beneath a tree,
I stir my ice cream back to liquid
then tip the spoon up into my mouth,
tasting this moment,
drinking in
the melty sweet cream of this day.

June

18

THE BALL GAME

Buggies wobble up the laneway as the game begins.
I wait
in the field,
trying to look fierce,
my hands sweaty
for fear
the ball will come my way.
It always does.

"Naomi!" I hear my name in every direction.
The ball drops from the sky,
sifts through my fingers.
"Naomi!" My name again,
but this time
with blame.
I chase the rolling ball, my hands stinging,
and throw it to Manassah, who knows
what to do with it.

I pick at the grass
as I wait my turn.
"Here's a heavy hitter," jokes Manassah
as I stumble to pick up the wooden bat.
The older boys laugh
and move in from the field.

Eye on the ball. Eye on the ball.
Swing.
Ball hits wood, *thwack*!
The "sweet spot," as Manassah calls it.
The ball flies through the sky like a freed bird,
up and over the wide-eyed boys,
bounces hard into the raspberry bushes.
I freeze, my arm shaking with the ring of the bat.
Lucinda looks at me and back to the adults,
then tiptoes through the garden for the ball.
Everyone starts to shout, "Naomi!"
I hike up my skirt
and run.

Finally,
it is too dark to see the ball.
We sit on the fresh-cut grass
and sing songs of praise
below
a pink sky.

THE BUGGY

Mam, tending to Lucinda's fever,
Manassah and Dat gone on ahead – the cart
stacked with lumber for the barn-raising.
"The pies…"
Mam remembers,
as the cart turns out of the lane.
"Naomi will have to drive the buggy."

I swallow hard, my heart galloping.
How I have longed for this day.
I've watched often enough but –
I can't ask how…can't
let this chance slip.

Long brush strokes
calming Pepper –
and me,
wondering how
to harness a horse.
Clip here? Buckle there?
Pull back, buckle again, again, and once more.
And again.

Esther and Jonah bounce on the seat,
eager for this freedom.
I grip the reins tight to steady my hands.
A slight quick pull – we start, slowly, down the lane –
right rein – right turn onto the road –
a sharp-pull *snap* and *chk* – the horse begins to trot.

Esther snuggles tight beside me,
Jonah leans back against my knees.
Secure in their closeness and trust,
I bite away sweat from my lip
and hold the reins firmly – assuring the horse,
I'm here.

Clop-clop, clop-clop.
Stalks of corn line the roadside
like a crowd for a parade,
waving
arms of green.

At the farm, Esther and Jonah leap out.
I peel myself off the hot, black seat
and step down onto jelly legs.
My friends run to see, whispering, giggling.
And I show them how
to harness a horse.

September

THE APPLE ORCHARD

I race out to the orchard,
away from Lucinda's voice.
The apple-y smell is everywhere
but deepest of all beneath the branches,
bending almost to the ground,
apples dripping toward the grass.

I scramble up a crooked trunk.
The tree's gnarled arms hide me from my chores:
peeling and slicing with Lucinda –
eight pies for Sunday's gathering.

Thunk! An apple knocks the branch below me.
"Mam's calling you, Naomi," Manassah shouts,
as he climbs behind the reins with Dat and Jonah.
At the end of the flat cart,
Esther crouches among rows of bushel baskets,
piled high with red and green apples.
They'll stop at the cider mill
then sell house-to-house in town.

The horses jolt forward;
stones snap and spew from beneath the wheels.
I chase after the cart and jump on the back.
Esther giggles and swings onto my lap.
The house shrinks smaller and smaller.
We hold each other tight,
her round, cool cheek against mine,
excited by our secret.

ROADSIDE STAND

Esther hides in the folds of Mam's skirt
as they wander up the lane to the house.
I glance back, wishing I were small enough to fit in
      those creases,
then return to my work.

Across the field, layers of gray-blue clouds dust the treetops;
mist fades the river to pastel.
But here, at the end of our lane,
the slanting autumn sun makes everything bright:
eggplants, pumpkins, peppers, zucchini and squash,
      cabbages and carrots,
the deepest purple, yellowest yellow, orangiest orange.
I lay the vegetables out in rows,
forming a tabletop garden,
then tighten my kerchief beneath my chin
and wait.

A car pulls over, churning dust into the air.
I turn back to the farm:
Lucinda bent over in the garden,
David and Manassah pouring potatoes into baskets,
Esther on the swing while Mam hangs out the wash.
No one runs to help.

The woman's heels click, then stop, as she chooses:
two pie pumpkins, three peppers, one jar of apple
      butter, a purple cabbage.
I add the numbers with my pencil and paper,
… my skirt flaps in the wind …
five plus five,
… blossoms of wild carrot tickle my ankles …
carry the one,
…cars whoosh by …
no, carry the two,
… she checks her watch ….

I clear my throat.
"That would be five dollars and fifty cents."
My words are white in the cold air.

As the car pulls away,
David sets two more baskets of potatoes in front
      of the table.
I lower my head
and smile,
then tighten my kerchief beneath my chin
and wait for another car.

THE BAKERY

Tumbling out of the buggy,
Esther runs to catch up with Mam.
I walk heel-against-toe, heel-against-toe,
stepping across the pale grass, crisp with frost.
The sky is white.
Dat says we may get snow today.

Warm yeasty air
and the tinkling of a tiny gold bell above the door
welcome me in.
Bran muffins, coffee cake,
cookies with raisins, and cookies with oats,
cream-filled donuts, and Chelsea buns,
lined up in boxes on white, painted shelves.

Lucinda and Almeda stand at a counter,
sprinkling brown sugar onto strips of dough.
Almeda opens a plumpy white hand,
caked thick with flour,
and gives us each a ball of dough and a smile.
Esther stuffs hers into her mouth.
I hold mine close to my nose, breathing in
the warmth and sweetness.

Back in the buggy,
the sky shakes out the first snow of the year.
Esther squeals.
Mam hands me the reins, pats my hand,
looks out to the road.
Flakes of sugary fluff,
whirling, twirling,
land on my cheeks,
still flushed and hot from the bakery,
and quickly melt away.

December

CHRISTMAS MORNING

Warm beneath my cotton quilt,
I thank the Lord for this day.
My nose is as cold as the windows;
panes thick with frost.
Wind whistles through the cracks,
leaving snow to settle in the corners.

I creak down the wooden stairs,
deeper and deeper into the sights and smells
of Christmas morning:
a pot of oatmeal bubbling on the stove,
sizzling eggs and bacon,
jam-jams and popcorn balls on the counter,
Jonah and Manassah stuffing their mouths with candy.
Esther coos down at her gift –
the yellow-haired doll from the store,
finally home in Esther's arms.

I take my place at the table and open my shoebox.
At first, only the fresh scent of an orange,
but then, my nose deep in the box,
smells of peppermint twists, peach chewy candies,
Mam's chocolate caramels.

"This one's for you, Naomi."
I look up from my shoebox as Dat hands me my gift.
It's the red View-Master.
And four cardboard circles:
Lake Louise, Pennsylvania, China, Bethlehem.
I drop *Bethlehem* into the slot:
blue, blue skies, donkeys and camels, houses made of
sand.

At church,
Dat leads us in song;
our voices follow:
"Stille Nacht, Heilige Nacht."
I think of the tiny pictures of Bethlehem
as I sing the story of a faraway world.

I thank the Lord for this day.

Flavors

Mennonites are famous for their delicious baked goods. The following recipes — one for each month of the year — are inspired by Mennonite tradition and call for fresh, seasonal ingredients.

Because much of the pleasure in baking comes from sharing the experience with someone you love, these recipes were especially created with children in mind.
All have been coded for their degree of difficulty with this small bonnet symbol

With all cooking, whether easy or challenging, always have an adult with you.

= easy. You can make most of this recipe by yourself and ask an adult to put it in the oven when needed.

= a bit more difficult. Have an adult help you with some steps, especially if using a mixer or chopping fruit.

= more challenging. You and an adult can do this one together.

OATMEAL AND EVERYTHING COOKIES

½ cup butter, softened
¾ cup brown sugar, firmly packed
¼ cup white sugar
1 egg
1 tablespoon milk
1 teaspoon vanilla extract
1 cup all-purpose flour
½ teaspoon baking soda
¼ teaspoon salt
1 ¼ cups large flake oats

Add-ins:
chocolate chips, butterscotch chips,
chopped nuts, raisins, dried cranberries

1. Preheat oven to 375°F (190°C).
2. Using a wooden spoon or mixer, cream butter and both sugars together.
3. Beat in egg, milk, and vanilla extract.
4. Whisk together flour, baking soda, and salt. Mix into batter well.
5. Add oats.
6. Stir in up to 1 ½ cups of any combination of the suggested add-ins.
7. Drop heaping spoonfuls of dough onto a greased or parchment-lined baking sheet, leaving about 2 inches between the cookies.
8. Bake for 9-10 minutes for chewy cookies or 12-13 minutes for crisp cookies.

January

TEA BISCUITS

¼ cup cold butter
1 ⅓ cups all-purpose flour
2 teaspoons white sugar
2 teaspoons baking powder
¼ teaspoon salt
½ cup milk
Extra flour for hands and board

1. Preheat oven to 400°F (200°C).
2. With a table knife, cut butter into small cubes. Add flour. Rub flour and butter together between your thumbs and fingers until it looks like large crumbs.
3. Mix in sugar, baking powder, and salt.
4. Stir in milk.
5. Rub flour on your hands and squeeze the dough into a ball, kneading it 3-4 times.
6. Pat down dough with your hands on a floured board or table until it is about a ½ inch thick.
7. Use a cookie cutter or lid to cut out circles, about 2-inches in diameter.
8. Place on an ungreased cookie sheet. Bake for 10-12 minutes, until golden.

February

MAPLE SYRUP BREAD PUDDING

¼ cup raisins

¼ cup maple syrup

6 slices white bread

2 eggs

1 cup milk

1 teaspoon vanilla extract

1 teaspoon cinnamon

¼ cup brown sugar, firmly packed

1. Preheat oven to 375°F (190°C).
2. Soak raisins in maple syrup.
3. Cut bread into cubes.
4. Place bread cubes in an 8-inch square baking dish, greased.
5. In a bowl, whisk together eggs, milk, vanilla extract, cinnamon, and brown sugar.
6. Fold the egg mixture into the bread cubes until the bread is soaked. If using stale bread, let it soak for 30 minutes.
7. Stir in the soaked raisins and maple syrup.
8. Bake uncovered for 35-40 minutes.
9. Serve warm, drizzled with more maple syrup.

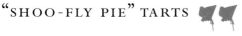

"SHOO-FLY PIE" TARTS

12 tart shells

Liquid:

½ teaspoon baking soda

¼ cup molasses

½ cup warm water

Crumbs:

⅔ cup all-purpose flour

½ cup brown sugar, firmly packed

¼ teaspoon cinnamon

⅓ cup butter

1. Preheat oven to 375°F (190°C).
2. Stir baking soda into molasses. Let it stand for 10-15 minutes until it becomes slightly foamy and lighter in color.
3. Stir in warm water.
4. In a separate bowl, mix together flour, brown sugar, cinnamon, and butter with a fork or fingers to make crumbs.
5. Pour enough liquid mixture into tart shells to cover the bottom. Sprinkle half the crumbs over the liquid. Pour the remaining liquid into the tarts and cover with the rest of the crumbs.
6. Bake on a parchment-covered tray for 15-20 minutes until set and golden brown.

March

April

STRAWBERRY-RHUBARB CUSTARD CRISP

3 cups rhubarb
1 cup strawberries
1 egg
1 ¾ cups white sugar
1 cup sour cream
⅓ cup all-purpose flour

Sugar Topping:
1 cup all-purpose flour
¾ cup brown sugar, firmly packed
½ cup butter, softened

1. Preheat oven to 375°F (190°C).
2. Clean and chop rhubarb and strawberries into bite-sized pieces and set aside.
3. In a large bowl, beat egg.
4. Mix in sugar, sour cream, and flour.
5. Gently stir in fruit.
6. Pour into 8-inch square baking dish.
7. In another bowl, mix flour and brown sugar for topping with a fork.
8. With your fingers or a fork, mix in butter until crumbly.
9. Pour topping over fruit mixture and spread it evenly over the top.
10. Bake for 40-45 minutes or until topping is golden brown.

VANILLA ICE CREAM IN A CAN WITH STRAWBERRIES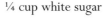

¼ cup white sugar
1 teaspoon vanilla extract
2 cups table cream (18%)

Small coffee can (or metal can with lid)
Larger metal can with lid
Lots of ice
½ cup coarse salt

1. Stir together sugar, vanilla extract, and cream.
2. Pour mixture into a small can and seal the lid tightly.
3. Place this can in the freezer for 30 minutes.
4. Set the small can in the larger can and fill the larger can with ice and salt.
5. Seal this lid tightly.
6. Roll, shake, and kick the can for 30-40 minutes or until ice cream is hardened.
7. Rinse salt off the can.
8. Serve your creamy ice cream with fresh strawberries (see below).

Strawberries with Ice Cream
1. Clean strawberries and cut into quarters.
2. Sprinkle 1 tablespoon of white sugar over berries and stir to coat.
3. Let stand for 10 minutes to draw out juice.
4. Serve over ice cream.

May

June

PEACH AND BERRY CRUMBLE

6 cups peaches, peeled and sliced
2 cups blueberries or raspberries
2 tablespoons all-purpose flour
¼ cup white sugar

Topping:

¾ cups rolled oats
⅔ cup brown sugar, firmly packed
½ cup all-purpose flour
½ cup melted butter
½ teaspoon cinnamon

1. Preheat oven to 350°F (180°C).
2. In a large bowl, mix peaches and berries with flour and sugar.
3. Gently stir to coat fruit.
4. Pour fruit mixture into an 8-inch square baking dish.
5. In another bowl, mix topping ingredients with a fork.
6. Sprinkle topping mixture evenly over fruit.
7. Bake for 45 minutes or until peaches are tender and topping is bubbly and golden brown.

DUTCH APPLE PIE

9-inch unbaked pie crust (see below)
½ cup brown sugar, firmly packed
½ cup white sugar
2 tablespoons all-purpose flour
3-4 cups apples, peeled and sliced in large chunks
½ cup table cream (18%)
½ teaspoon cinnamon
1 tablespoon butter, softened

1. Preheat oven to 450°F (230°C).
2. Combine brown sugar, white sugar, and flour. Spread ⅓ of this mixture in the bottom of the pie crust.
3. Line apple chunks in circles around inside of pie crust, packing them in quite tightly, until crust is filled.
4. Sprinkle remaining sugar mixture over apples.
5. Drizzle cream over the sugar and apples.
6. Sprinkle cinnamon and dab butter over the apples.
7. Bake for 15 minutes, then turn oven down to 350°F (180°C) and continue baking for another 35 minutes or until apples are tender.

Pie Crust:

1 cup all-purpose flour
Pinch of salt
½ cup vegetable shortening
2 tablespoons water

1. Use two table knives to cut flour and salt into shortening. Continue until mixture is the size of small peas.
2. Gradually add two tablespoons of water.
3. Mix gently with fingertips. Form into a ball.
4. Spread flour on a rolling pin and on a clean surface. Roll the dough out gently to form a 12-13-inch circle.
5. Carefully lift the dough into a 9-inch pie plate.
6. Cut around the outside of the dough, leaving an edge hanging over the side of the pie plate. Pinch the dough around the edges.

September

October

APPLE BLOSSOMS

For each apple blossom, you will need:

1 package puff pastry dough, thawed
1 tablespoon brown sugar, firmly packed
1 teaspoon margarine
¼ teaspoon cinnamon
1 teaspoon all-purpose flour
½ apple, peeled and chopped
Egg white

1. Preheat oven to 400°F (200°C).
2. Cut puff pastry dough into eight pieces.
3. Roll out one piece of dough with a rolling pin to make a pancake shape.
4. Put the brown sugar, margarine, cinnamon, flour, and apples in a plastic zip bag and shake well.
5. Pour apple mixture onto the dough.
6. Wrap edges of the dough together and twist.
7. Brush egg white on the outside to make it stick.
8. Repeat steps 2-6 for each apple blossom.
9. Place on a parchment-lined tray and bake apple blossoms for 30 minutes.
10. Serve warm with ice cream.

PUMPKIN MUFFINS

2 eggs
1 cup white sugar
⅓ cup oil
⅓ cup apple sauce
1 cup canned or fresh pumpkin purée
1 ½ cups all-purpose flour
1 teaspoon cinnamon
1 teaspoon baking powder
1 teaspoon baking soda
½ teaspoon salt
1 cup chocolate chips or raisins.

1. Preheat oven to 375°F (190°C).
2. In a large bowl, beat eggs. Beat in sugar, oil, apple sauce, and pumpkin.
3. In a separate bowl, mix flour, cinnamon, baking powder, baking soda, and salt.
4. Fold the dry ingredients into the wet ingredients.
5. Add chocolate chips or raisins.
6. Divide the batter into 12 muffin cups.
7. Bake for 20-25 minutes, until a toothpick inserted comes out clean.

WHOOPIE PIES

1 ounce semi-sweet chocolate

½ cup butter, softened

1 cup brown sugar, firmly packed

1 egg

1 teaspoon vanilla extract

1 cup buttermilk

1 ¾ cups all-purpose flour

¾ cups cocoa

1 ½ teaspoon baking soda

½ teaspoon baking powder

½ teaspoon salt

Filling:

1 cup butter, softened

2 cups icing sugar

1 ½ teaspoons vanilla extract

½ teaspoon milk

2 cups marshmallow cream

1. Preheat oven to 350°F (180°C).
2. Gradually melt the chocolate. Let it cool slightly.
3. Using a wooden spoon, cream butter and brown sugar together.
4. Add egg, vanilla extract, cooled chocolate, and buttermilk. Beat well, scraping sides and bottom of bowl.
5. In a separate bowl, whisk together the remaining dry ingredients.
6. Add dry ingredients to wet mixture gradually, mixing well.
7. Using a small scoop, drop batter onto parchment-lined baking sheets, leaving about 2 inches between the pies.
8. Bake for 12-15 minutes until tops crack slightly and a toothpick inserted comes out clean.
9. Let the pies cool completely before adding filling.

1. Using a wooden spoon or mixer, cream butter and sugar together.
2. Add vanilla extract and milk, blend in.
3. Add marshmallow cream and beat well.
4. Spread filling generously on the flat side of a whoopie pie. Place another half on top and gently press together.

CARAMEL POPCORN

12 cups plain popped popcorn (about ½ cup popping corn)

1 cup brown sugar, firmly packed

½ cup butter, softened

¼ cup corn syrup

½ teaspoon salt

1 teaspoon vanilla extract

½ teaspoon baking soda

1. Preheat oven at 350°F (180°C).
2. In a small saucepan, heat brown sugar, butter, corn syrup, and salt until bubbly.
3. Let it cool slightly and then add vanilla extract and baking soda.
4. Pour over popcorn and toss until coated.
5. Spread on a foil-lined tray and bake for 7-10 minutes, turning often.
7. Remove from oven and continue turning as it cools.

November

December